YAS

FRIENDS
OF ACPL

W9-AXI-096

ILLEGAL IMMIGRATION

ILLEGAL

IMMIGRATION

BY KAREN KENNEY

Content Consultant
Kwao Amegashie
Attorney at Law
Minneapolis, Minnesota

ABDO
Publishing Company

CREDITS

Editor: Paula Lewis
Cover Design: Becky Daum
Interior Design: Lindaanne Donohoe

Library of Congress Cataloging-in-Publication Data
Kenney, Karen Latchana.
  Illegal immigration / Karen Kenney.
    p. cm.—(Essential viewpoints)
  Includes bibliographical references and index.
  ISBN 978-1-59928-861-1
  1. Illegal aliens—United States—Juvenile literature. 2. Emigration and immigration—Juvenile literature. I. Title.

  JV6483.K46 2008
  325.73 dc22

                                    2007013881

TABLE OF CONTENTS

Immigration and Customs Enforcement police stand guard at the entrance of a Swift & Company meatpacking plant.

A National Raid

*I*t began in the early hours on Tuesday, December 12, 2006. U.S. Immigration and Customs Enforcement (ICE) officials marched into Swift & Company meatpacking plants in Texas, Nebraska, Utah, Colorado, Iowa, and Minnesota.

Armed with military weapons, they locked down the plants, separated groups of workers, and began interviewing them.

What were the officials looking for? Officials believed that illegal aliens had obtained the Social Security numbers of U.S. citizens through criminal organizations in order to gain U.S. employment. The ICE officials were searching for illegal immigrants who were working in the plants using false identification.

"Part of a comprehensive immigration plan is to give employers the tools necessary to determine whether or not the workers they're looking for are here legally in America. And we've got such a plan—Basic Pilot . ... It's working."[2]

—*President George W. Bush, July 5, 2006*

Concerned that there was a large-scale identity theft scheme at the plants, ICE officials had obtained search warrants. Of the 1,282 illegal immigrants, 65 were arrested for criminal violations, some of which involved identity theft. According to Michael Chertoff, Secretary of Homeland Security:

> *Violations of our immigration laws and privacy rights often go hand in hand. Enforcement actions like this one protect the privacy rights of innocent Americans while striking a blow against illegal immigration.*[1]

As a result of this raid, almost 1,300 workers were arrested. Production was halted for the entire day in these plants. Some detainees were transported to outlying cities. Some were unable to contact friends or family to make arrangements for their children to be picked up from school. Others were separated from their American spouses and children, forcing families to decide if they would live separately or reunite in their home countries. The United Food and Commercial Workers Union (UFCW) and attorneys represented the rights of these workers. However, they were denied contact with those who were arrested.

The Need for Unskilled Workers

It is unpleasant work. Meatpacking plants, also known as slaughterhouses, process beef, pork, and poultry. The working conditions are cold, messy, and dangerous. According to J. Patrick Boyle, president of the American Meat Institute, the industry attracts foreign-born workers "because we pay, on average, nearly $25,000 a year plus benefits for jobs that require no formal training or prior experience."[3] This income may seem low and the type of work undesirable to many Americans. But, the pay and working environment are much better here than what many immigrants would find in their native country.

Changes in U.S. society have affected the number of unskilled workers available for these kinds of jobs. In 1960, half of American men dropped out of high school to begin working. Today, less than 10 percent do so. Nearly 185,000 jobs are created annually in the construction industry, but employers cannot find enough U.S. workers to fill these jobs. The restaurant industry is also growing. Between 2005 and 2015, jobs in this field are expected to grow by 15 percent, while the American-born workforce is expected to grow by only 10 percent.

Sam Rovit, the president of Swift & Company, said that Swift had never knowingly hired unauthorized workers in its plants. According to Rovit, Swift had been complying with the Basic Pilot Program since 1997. This program is a voluntary online verification system. Employers can confirm a new employee's eligibility by comparing the personal information they provide against federal databases.

While the raids slowed production only slightly, Rovit said it could cost millions of dollars to replace lost workers. He also said if the raids continued, it could bring "a shrinking in the industry, because there is not enough labor to go around."[4]

These raids represent a prominent issue in the immigration debate in the United States. Millions of illegal immigrants are unlawfully employed nationwide. According to the Pew Hispanic Center, nearly 12 million unauthorized immigrants lived in the United States in 2006. Many illegal immigrants take

"The workers caught in this vice are victims of a failed immigration system. It's time for the federal government to stop victimizing workers and reform our immigration system. ... Worksite raids with armed agents are not the answer to the nationwide call for immigration reform. America deserves a humane, systematic and comprehensive immigration policy immediately."[5]

—Mark Lauritsen, international vice president and director of the Food Processing, Packing, and Manufacturing division of the UFCW

3 1833 05625 8871

the low-paying jobs that most Americans do not want. These jobs include low-skilled labor on farms or construction sites and in factories, restaurants, and other industries. Illegal immigrants have become part of the American economy. Employers hire them as a way for their businesses to survive and thrive in the United States.

> "The ICE investigation conducted around the Swift & Company plants discovered a number of cases of suspected identity theft, which is supported by these indictments. This investigation has shown how individual U.S. citizens are tragically affected when aliens steal identities to obtain work. The aliens charged today will have their day in court. If convicted, they'll first serve their sentences before they're removed to their countries of origin."[6]
>
> —*John Chakwin, special agent in charge of the ICE Office of Investigations in Dallas, Texas*

LIVING AND WORKING IN THE UNITED STATES

Under current law, illegal immigrants are not legally allowed to work and live in the United States. The U.S. Citizenship and Immigration Services' Web site explains the two main methods by which a foreign-born person can gain lawful permanent residence (also known as a Green Card).

One method is through a family member. This can be by marriage to a U.S. citizen or through sponsorship by a family member who is a U.S. citizen. The second method is through employment. An employer can

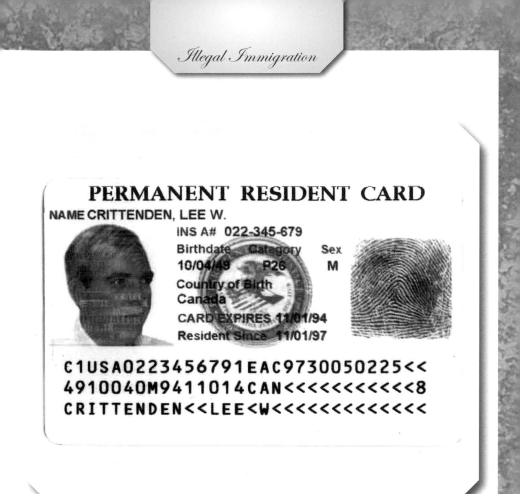

An example of the Immigration and Naturalization Services' new Green Card. It is designed to be counterfeit-resistant and incorporates many security features.

sponsor a foreign-born person by vouching that the person has skills needed by the employer. In addition to these two methods, a diversity lottery distributes 50,000 permanent U.S. resident visas each year to countries with low rates of U.S. immigration.

To become a citizen of the United States, a foreign-born person must:

- Live for a continuous specified period of time within the United States.

- Be able to read, write, and speak English.

- Understand U.S. history and government.

- Be of good moral character.

- Believe in the principles of the U.S. Constitution.

- Have positive feelings about the United States.

HEART OF THE CONTROVERSY

For many, the legal path to American citizenship is overwhelming and seemingly impossible. Many people believe the U.S. immigration system is outdated and overly restrictive. For instance, consider a legal permanent resident of the United States who is of Mexican origin. It may take up to 13 years for the legal permanent resident to bring his or her spouse to the United States. The immigration process takes time, money, knowledge of English, and an understanding of the U.S. legal process.

Others believe that U.S. immigration laws are not restrictive enough. Some groups and lawmakers believe illegal immigrants should be convicted as federal felons.

They would then be denied health care, social services, and education.

For example, in 1994, California residents approved Proposition 187. This proposition made illegal immigrants ineligible for public social services, public health care services, and public school education. The proposition also required state and local agencies to report suspected illegal immigrants to the state and federal governments. It also made it a felony to manufacture, sell, or use false citizenship or residence documents.

Many factors contribute to illegal immigration in the United States. Employers need laborers. But, employers do not have the means to detect false identification cards and Social Security numbers. Illegal immigrants find other ways to enter the country. They either enter legally through a temporary pass or visa or by illegally crossing the borders.

Why Leave Mexico?

Why, when Mexico has the healthiest economy in Latin America, do millions of its people want to leave and come to the United States? There is a lot of money in Mexico. The issue is how that wealth is distributed.

ECLAC is the Economic Commission for Latin America and the Caribbean. It reports that only six countries in the world outside of Africa have a more unequal distribution of wealth than Mexico.

The 1996 annual World Bank report states that, in Mexico, 25 percent of Mexicans earn less than $2 (U.S.) per day. And, 17 percent earn less than $1. This translates to almost half of Mexicans being poor.

Until Mexico can provide work opportunities and a livable wage for its citizens, Mexicans will continue to enter the United States seeking a better quality of life.

Illegal immigrants are in the United States. They participate in American society. How should the government handle illegal immigrants who are already living in the United States? How should the government prevent more illegal immigrants from entering the United States?

To begin to answer these questions, it is important to understand the ways illegal immigration affects U.S. economy and culture—both positively and negatively. Why do illegal immigrants come to the United States? How do illegal immigrants enter the country and find employment? Who hires illegal immigrants? Does their employment affect wage levels for U.S. citizens and legal residents? And when, in a country that was founded by immigrants, did the term "illegal immigrant" become a part of the modern vocabulary?

Illegal immigrant day laborers looking for work gather at a street corner where potential employers stop to hire workers.

Approximately 12 million immigrants entered the United States through Ellis Island from 1892 to 1954.

U.S. IMMIGRATION AND LEGISLATION

The history of immigration and the formation of the United States are intertwined. The original inhabitants of North America, the Native Americans, lived in tribes across the continent. Immigrants developed central North America into the

nation now known as the United States. The first
European settlements formed in the 1500s and 1600s
along the eastern Atlantic seaboard. Immigrant groups
began arriving in North America as early as the 1600s.

Immigrants made the difficult journey by ship, often
in dreadful conditions. Countless people died along
the way. These immigrants fled their home countries
for several reasons. Religious
groups came for the freedom of
worship. The desire for better
economic opportunities also
brought settlers to North
American shores. The majority of
these first settlers were English.
They formed the basis of U.S.
government, law, language, and a
tradition of religious freedom.

Irish, German, Dutch, French,
Swiss, Swedish, Polish, and other
European immigrants also arrived.
They freely entered the country.
There were no immigration laws.
America was thought of as a wide,
open land of limitless opportunity and freedoms.
Colonies were established and thrived in the new land.

Land of Opportunity

Leaflets, or advertisements,
were created to persuade
English citizens to emigrate
from England to America.
These leaflets promised
new opportunities and fruit-
ful lands for farming. They
also offered advice to new
settlers. A leaflet printed in
1622 listed the following
household items needed for
a family of six people:
- One Iron Pot
- One kettle
- One large frying pan
- One gridiron
- Two skillets
- One spit
- Platters, dishes, spoones
  [*sic*] of wood[1]

In 1619, the first Africans were brought against their will to Virginia to provide slave labor on plantations. Thousands of unemployed and homeless men who were unable to pay passage to North America agreed to work without wages for a number of years as indentured servants in exchange for their trip. Industries grew throughout the nineteenth century. Factories, manufacturing plants, and timberlands needed workers. Immigrants came in huge numbers to satisfy those needs.

In the 1700s, North America was a land not only of immigrants—but a land of people born on American soil of immigrant parents. The American colonies declared their independence from Great Britain in 1776. This was followed by the American Revolutionary War. By 1788, the U.S. Constitution was ratified.

The Introduction of Immigration Legislation

The California Gold Rush began in 1848. This brought Chinese immigrants to California. By 1870, approximately 100,000 Chinese immigrants had arrived. Many lived in self-contained communities, such as Chinatown in San Francisco. They were valued for their labor on the railroads and in factories.

At first, the Chinese took jobs that were unwanted

and accepted lower pay. When jobs became difficult to find, fear and hostility grew toward the Chinese. Many believed that the Chinese were taking away their jobs and forcing the wages down. This led to the Chinese Exclusion Act of 1882.

This was the first major U.S. immigration legislation. It suspended immigration of Chinese laborers and stopped Chinese naturalization. The act also allowed for Chinese people to be legally sent out of the country.

STATUE OF LIBERTY

Dedicated in 1886, the Statue of Liberty was a gift to the United States from France as a symbol of friendship and democracy. The Statue of Liberty was assembled on Bedloe's Island (since renamed Liberty Island), facing the New York harbor. With her majestic robes and uplifted arm with glowing torch, she symbolized the hopes and dreams for a new life to immigrants from around the world.

In 1883, Emma Lazarus wrote the poem "The New Colossus." In 1903, 16 years after Lazarus's death, the poem was included on the plaque at the base of the statue. The poem captures the immigrant ideals of the time:

The New Colossus

...A mighty woman with a torch, whose flame....

From her beacon–hand

Glows world–wide welcome...

"Give me your tired, your poor,

Your huddled masses yearning to breathe free,

The wretched refuse of your teeming shore.

Send these, the homeless, tempest–tost to me,

I lift my lamp beside the golden door!"[2]

First Federal Immigration Station

Samuel Ellis was the first private owner of the island that became known as Ellis Island. The island was eventually sold to the federal government in 1808 for $10,000. It has retained the name Ellis Island.

On January 1, 1892, the immigration station opened on Ellis Island. The first immigrant to enter through the station was 15-year-old Annie Moore from County Cork, Ireland.

Between 1892 and 1922, approximately 16 million immigrants entered the United States through New York's Ellis Island. After proving their identity and finding a relative to vouch for them, 98 percent of the immigrants were admitted to the United States.

A record number of 11,747 immigrants passed through Ellis Island on April 17, 1907. The island was officially closed as an immigration station in November 1954.

LEGISLATING IMMIGRATION

Immigration policy excluded people based on certain factors. Criminals, prostitutes, the physically and mentally ill, and people who were likely to need public aid were denied entrance to the United States.

Customs agents also refused entry to lunatics and the sick. The term "illegal immigrant" was meaningless.

The Immigration Act of 1891 set up the first comprehensive law to control immigration and direct deportation. It also established the Bureau of Immigration. The National Origins Act of 1924 established a quota system and numerical limit on immigration. This law limited the number of European immigrants to 150,000 per year and barred Japanese immigration. The quota system allowed set percentages of immigrants to enter from certain countries. This percentage was based on the proportion of national origin groups represented in the 1890 census, which determined that most Americans were of northern and western European descent. Because of this, the quota system favored immigrants from those areas of Europe.

The Immigration and Nationality Act of 1965 ended the quota system and set a uniform limit of 20,000 immigrants per Eastern Hemisphere country. In addition, a seven-category preference system based on family unification and skills was established. This law also, for the first time, set a limit on immigrants from the Western Hemisphere (including Mexico).

A close-up view of the Statue of Liberty

Three major pieces of immigration legislation were enacted between 1980 and 1990.

The Refugee Act of 1980:

- Set up the first system and procedure for admitting refugees to the United States.

- Removed refugees as a category in the preference system.

- Created an asylum or refugee status for immigrants.

The Immigration Reform and Control Act (IRCA) of 1986:

- Instituted penalties for employers who knowingly hired illegal immigrants.

- Increased border enforcement.

- Created two programs to grant legal status to illegal immigrants.

The Immigration Act of 1990:

- Increased immigration limits by 40 percent.

- Tripled employment-based immigration (emphasizing education and skills).

- Granted more visas to countries with little immigration to the United States between 1985 and 1990.

- Expanded the refugee policy to include people fleeing natural disasters and war.

From 1996 to Today

In 1996, the Illegal Immigration Reform and Immigrant Responsibility Act passed. This law:

- Emphasized enforcement of and penalties for violating immigration law.

- Set restrictions on the public benefits that immigrants could receive.

- Increased U.S. border enforcement.
- Set up three electronic employment verification systems to assist employers in hiring legal workers.

In 2006, the Secure Fence Act was signed by President George W. Bush. This act focuses on the border between the United States and Mexico. The act:

- Allows for the expanded construction of fencing along the border.
- Increases lighting, vehicle barriers, and checkpoints.
- Increases the technology used to detect illegal border crossings, such as cameras, satellites, and unmanned aerial vehicles.

Today, people in the United States are debating comprehensive immigration reform. They want to deal with border security and the number of illegal immigrants living within those borders. In the meantime, illegal immigrants continue to find their way to U.S. soil.

Amnesty

The 1986 Amnesty Act (or law) was valid for one year. It legalized the status of those living illegally in the United States since January 1, 1982. This law granted legal residency to 2 million people and benefited many Mexicans and other aliens.

This 14-mile U.S.-Mexico border fence separates San Diego and Tijuana, Mexico. The homes are in Tijuana. This section will be the western end of the fence when the 700 miles of fencing is built between California and Texas.

A group of men on their way to a drop-off spot where they will illegally cross on foot into the United States near Arivaca, Arizona.

ILLEGAL IMMIGRANTS

With the legislation of the late 1980s and 1990s and the terrorist attacks of September 11, 2001, U.S. border security has tightened incredibly. Penalties for hiring illegal immigrants have increased. Immigration reform is often in the news.

How do illegal immigrants still enter through the U.S. borders? Where do the majority of illegal immigrants come from?

Today, an estimated 27 million foreign-born residents are in the United States. Of these, almost 17 million are legal residents, while the balance are here illegally. Between the years 2000 and 2004, the number of illegal immigrants increased by 408,000 people per year. That number is comparable to the rates of immigration in the early 1900s, when immigration was mostly unrestricted. In the early 1900s, most immigrants were of European descent. Today, most of the illegal immigrants are from the third-world countries of Latin America and Asia.

The United States shares a 2,000-mile (3,000-km) border with Mexico. Certain ports of entry, including airports, can be strictly regulated through immigration and customs offices. However, many miles of the border are unoccupied, and the harsh terrain is impossible to guard completely.

According to a Department of Homeland Security report, Mexico

Third-world Country

Countries that are under-developed economically and experience poverty and high birth rates are considered to be third-world countries. These countries often exist in Latin America, Africa, and Asia and rely on aid from economically advanced countries.

was the leading source of unauthorized immigrants as of January 2005. Nearly 6 million Mexicans were living illegally in the United States at the time of the report. People from El Salvador, Guatemala, India, and China accounted for a total of 1.4 million unauthorized immigrants. The remaining illegal immigrants come from countries such as Korea, the Philippines, Honduras, Brazil, and Vietnam.

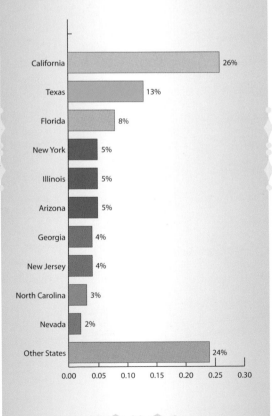

Unauthorized Immigrants

When unauthorized immigrants arrive in the United States, where do they live? The following chart is based on estimates for 2005 from the Department of Homeland Security.

State	Percentage
California	26%
Texas	13%
Florida	8%
New York	5%
Illinois	5%
Arizona	5%
Georgia	4%
New Jersey	4%
North Carolina	3%
Nevada	2%
Other States	24%

0.00   0.05   0.10   0.15   0.20   0.25   0.30

MODES OF ENTRY

Immigrants can enter the United States legally with visas or passes that allow them to stay for a certain period of time. Visas are distributed to foreign students, travelers, and people who are conducting business in the United States. Border Crossing Cards are given to Mexicans to travel across the border to shop or visit the United States for a day. The recipients of this card are required to prove that they have binding ties to Mexico and, therefore, need to return.

People who violate the terms of their temporary visa and remain in the United States beyond their allowed time are considered to be "unlawfully present." Once this occurs, the U.S. government considers them to be illegal immigrants. According to a May 2006 report by the Pew Hispanic Center, approximately 40 to 50 percent of illegal immigrants (4.5 to 6 million people) entered the country legally, but are considered to be unlawfully present, having exceeded their allowed time in the United States. The Border Crossing Card violators account for 250,000 to 500,000 people.

The remaining 50 to 60 percent of illegal immigrants entered without a U.S. Immigration and

Anti-American

According to a report by the Center for Immigration Studies, 48 foreign-born terrorists were arrested between 1993 and 2001. Of those 48 terrorists, 16 were in the United States on temporary visas (primarily tourist), 17 were legal residents or naturalized U.S. citizens, and 12 were illegal aliens who had applied for asylum.

Customs inspection. It is difficult to estimate the number of illegal immigrants who enter the country this way. There is no way to officially track these people as they evade customs officials. Some enter by hiding in vehicles, such as cargo trucks, that cross through official ports of entry along the border. Others hike across the Arizona desert, wade across the Rio Grande River, or use tunnels that are dug underneath the border. For all of these methods, it is either dangerous or costly—and usually both.

Human smugglers, also known as "coyotes," are paid a fee to either drive illegal immigrants across the border and deliver them to U.S. cities or guide them by foot across the border. From 1982 to 1992, the price to hire a coyote was approximately $400 per person. By 2007, the price ranged between $2,000 and $3,600. It is a dangerous business for both the coyote and the illegal alien. The coyote could face a serious jail sentence if caught smuggling illegal aliens across the border. Illegal aliens face the possibility of extreme conditions. Coyotes may leave illegal immigrants for hours in truck trailers that are very hot and do not have a source of fresh air and water.

Some illegal immigrants travel through long tunnels dug underneath the U.S.-Mexico border. One

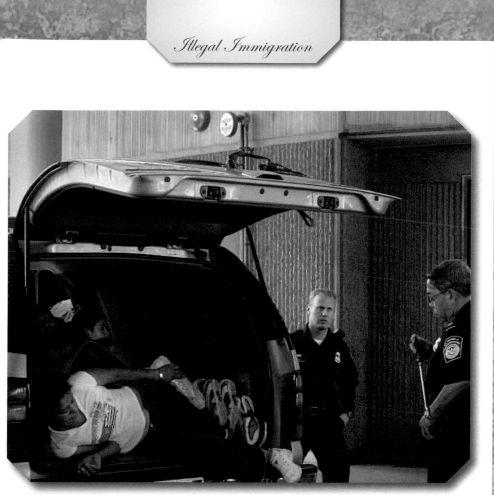

U.S. Customs and Border Protection officers find a group of 14 people who were being smuggled from Tijuana, Mexico, into San Diego, California, in the rear passenger and cargo areas of a van.

sophisticated tunnel connecting a Mexicali, Mexico, home to a house in Calexico, California, was found in 2005. The tunnel was three feet (1 m) wide and five feet (1.6 m) high. It had a tile floor, electric and ventilation systems, wooden walls, and even security cameras.

Loss of Life

On May 14, 2003, Tyrone M. Williams parked his milk truck at a truck stop near Victoria, Texas. Then he drove away in the cab of his truck, leaving behind his 18-wheeler trailer. Inside that trailer were 74 illegal aliens—19 died due to suffocation. During his trial, Williams' passenger in the cab testified that Williams had ignored the banging of the passengers. The temperatures reached as high as 173° F (78° C). Passengers were suffering in the airless trailer from dehydration. Williams was found guilty on 58 counts, which included transporting resulting in death.

The illegal immigrants suffer the most from the experience of traveling into the unknown with complete strangers. A 2005 Government Accountability Office (GAO) report stated that the number of border deaths has doubled from 1995 to 2005. Some deaths were caused by heat exhaustion and dehydration (the lack of water) while crossing the desert. Others died from the lack of oxygen and extreme temperatures while locked in vehicles.

Illegal immigrants, as the population numbers show, are still willing to take the risk to enter the United States illegally. What happens when they are in the United States and have settled into communities? What issues do they face? How do Americans and legal residents feel about their new neighbors?

IMMIGRANTS' RIGHTS PROJECT

The American Civil Liberties Union (ACLU) is active in the debate regarding illegal immigrants.

According to their Web site, one of their founding principles is to defend immigrants' rights. In 1987, the ACLU initiated the Immigrants' Rights Project (IRP). The goal is to protect the rights of illegal immigrants. This includes protection from discrimination and deportation. Another priority of IRP is to assert workers' rights. Chandra Bhatnagar, an ACLU attorney, states, "International human rights law requires the United States to apply its workplace protections equally and without discrimination based on immigration status."[1]

HUMANITARIAN EFFORTS

Humane Borders is a religious group that offers aid to illegal aliens crossing Arizona's Sonoran Desert. They have built more than 70 emergency water stations near the U.S.-Mexican border. These water stations help aliens stay alive as they try to enter the United States through the desert. Reverend Robin Hoover explained the group's mission by saying, "We want to take death out of the equation."[2]

In an unusual cooperation between the U.S. Border Patrol and the group, officers have guided Humane Borders to the best spots for their water tanks. As security has tightened on safer border crossing areas,

"The loss of life along our border and in the West Desert Corridor is deplorable and unacceptable. One of the best ways to protect lives is to better secure our border. With Operation Desert Safeguard, we will dramatically reduce the number of people attempting to illegally enter the United States through the Sonoran Desert area, and by so doing, we will be able to dramatically reduce the number of people who die attempting to cross that desert."[3]

—*U.S. Customs and Border Protection Commissioner Robert C. Bronner*

more aliens have attempted entering the United States through the desert.

Humane Borders was formed after a group of ranchers in Texas shot and killed aliens trying to cross the border. Outraged by the shootings, the volunteer group began their humanitarian efforts.

These mixed responses to border crossings parallel the mixed feelings over the immigration debate. As some groups push to close the borders, others fight to open them.

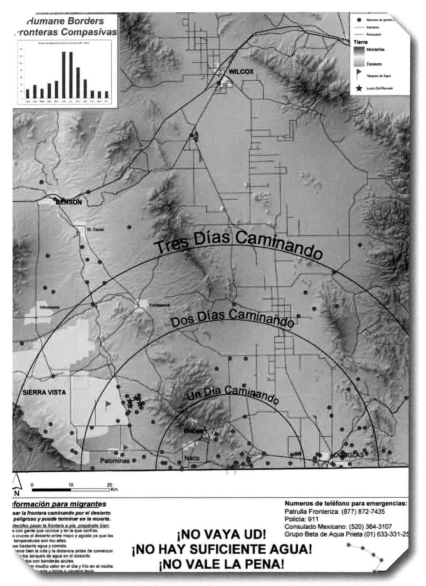

This 2006 Humane Borders poster shows a map marking migrant deaths. Mexico's National Commission for Human Rights agreed to print and distribute these to inform migrants of the dangers in the desert and to assist migrants in making responsible decisions.

Protesting the hiring of illegal immigrants

XENOPHOBIA, RACISM, OR CONCERNED CITIZENS?

he United States has had a history of xenophobia, the "fear or hatred of strangers or foreigners or of anything foreign or strange."[1] There is a fine line between racism and xenophobia, though both can apply to anti-immigrant feelings.

Even European groups had a difficult time in the early days of U.S. immigration. The early Irish immigrants, mostly peasants and farmers fleeing the effects of the Potato Famine, were generally poor and unskilled. The Irish arrived in large numbers to the United States between 1820 and 1920. They were often met with job discrimination and advertisements stating "No Irish Need Apply."

Italian, German, Polish, and Jewish people also experienced discrimination. Many Americans believed that these new immigrant groups would not assimilate or become part of the American culture. Some Americans voiced concerns that these immigrants would retain their original language and bring their foreign political issues to the United States.

Many Americans have deep feelings about the issue of illegal immigration. Many who strongly oppose it believe that illegal aliens should be punished and deported through removal proceedings. Others believe illegal immigrants will soon overpopulate the United States and damage the economy, culture, and environment. Still others believe that illegal aliens are criminals, as shown by their illegal presence.

And, there is an opposing point of view. Some Americans think that these beliefs are racist because much of the opposition is directed at illegal immigrants who are not Caucasian. These illegal immigrants are highly visible to the average American. As such, they are often blamed for lack of employment, low wages, or problems in their communities. Immigration supporters believe that the variety of cultures and skills immigrants bring to the United States are what has made this country so successful.

Groups Against Open Immigration

Today, there are organized groups who strongly oppose illegal immigration. These groups include Immigrations Human Cost, the Federation for American Immigration Reform (FAIR), and the Minuteman Project. Their opposition is based on:

- The legality of illegal immigrants' entry and residence in the United States.

- The economic and cultural effects that illegal immigrants have on the United States.

The fact that illegal immigrants break U.S. laws by illegally crossing the border, finding illegal employment, or using falsified identification documents are all major points. In a statement by Brenda Walker on the Immigrations Human Cost

Minuteman members protest migrant farm workers on private property in the rural part of Carmel Valley of San Diego.

Web site, she writes:

> *Perhaps it should be mentioned that part of the point of legal immigration, besides the issue of the simple fairness of taking a number and standing in line, is the inspection of prospective immigrants to keep out criminals, terrorists and those who have infectious diseases. ... Of course, a country that calls itself a "nation of laws" should be awarding its most valuable asset—citizenship—on the basis of an orderly queue, rather than selfish gatecrashing.*[2]

Some groups believe that the population of America is growing to dangerously high levels. These groups ask that immigration policies be enforced and reformed to control those numbers. They voice a concern that immigrants are taking over cities—forcing native-born Americans out. In a news release, FAIR president Dan Stein states:

> *If the president and others believe that the United States will be a better, more prosperous, more harmonious nation as a result of continued immigration-induced rapid population growth, let them articulate their case to the American public. If, on the other hand, they*

You Don't Speak for Me

Not all Hispanic-American citizens are sympathetic with the plight and goals of undocumented Hispanic immigrants. There are organized groups who oppose illegal immigration and want their opinions heard. One such group is You Don't Speak for Me (YDSFM).

The YDSFM group is comprised of Americans of Hispanic/Latino heritage and legal immigrants. Their principles are based on the following beliefs:

- All immigration should be done legally. Illegal immigration must be stopped.
- Illegal aliens should not be granted benefits or privileges. People who bypass the legal routes should not be rewarded with state or federal benefits.
- No amnesty should be given. Amnesty leads to increased illegal immigration.
- Build a high-security fence on the border. Allow local and state police officers to enforce immigration laws. Fine and/or jail employers who hire illegal aliens.
- Learn and speak English. All immigrants should learn the language and history of the United States.

value what is left of our open spaces, our environment and our natural resources, then they must develop policies that address the single largest source of population growth in the United States: immigration.[3]

Members of the Minuteman Project believe the future of the common culture of the country is at stake. They are concerned that the growth of legal and illegal immigration in the United States will result in a country with a mix of cultures. Groups such as the Minuteman Project believe that the foreign-born population in the United States will retain the language and culture of their home country and will divide the nation.

SUPPORT FOR CREATING A PATH TO CITIZENSHIP

In the spring of 2007, the American Friends Service Committee (AFSC) conducted a random telephone survey of 1,200 people across the United States.

Respondents were asked to rate various statements on a scale of 1 to 10, with 10 indicating complete agreement. The following is a sampling of the statements and the rating they received:

- *We are a nation of immigrants. (8.4)*
- *The nation's immigration system is broken. (8.03)*
- *Keeping families together should be a priority in our immigration policies. (7.74)*
- *Immigrants come to the U.S. to work, not to do us harm. (7.56)*
- *Building more fences on the border will not stop the flow of immigrants to the U.S. (6.90)*
- *Politicians blame illegal immigrants for our social problems to avoid handling real solutions to the nation's problems with jobs, education, and health care. (6.97)[4]*

Those surveyed were also asked several Yes/No/I Don't Know questions. Results showed that two-thirds of those surveyed support creating a path to citizenship for undocumented workers.

DIFFERENT SIDES OF THE FENCE

Supporters on both sides of the issue promote clearly defined arguments about illegal immigration. It is important to look at how the issue of illegal immigration becomes visible in communities and how it incites such strong emotions.

President Bush speaking on immigration reform to the
U.S. Chamber of Commerce

In Arizona, a U.S. Border Patrol agent pats down an illegal immigrant. Arizona has the greatest number of people illegally crossing along the U.S.-Mexico border.

CRIME, DRUGS, AND ILLEGAL IMMIGRANTS

Opinions are divided when it comes to the issue of illegal immigration and criminal activity. Some illegal immigrants are criminals. Some are involved in dangerous gangs. Some even smuggle drugs across the border. However, some American citizens also are involved with the drug trade. According to reports, immigrants are less likely to commit crimes than Americans. There is convincing evidence for both sides of this issue.

Does Illegal Immigration Raise Crime Rates?

Heather Mac Donald has a fellowship at the Manhattan Institute for Policy Research. She has written an article on crime and illegal immigrants. Mac Donald states that some of the most violent criminals are illegal aliens. Part of the problem, Mac Donald writes, is that violent criminals who are deported often return to the same American city. The local police departments, who recognize some of these returning criminals, cannot enforce immigration law. These "sanctuary policies" ban city employees, including local police, from reporting immigration violations to the federal authorities.

Mac Donald cites statistics that show the extent of the problem in southern California:

Special Order 40

In 1979, Special Order 40 was enacted by the Los Angeles Police Department (LAPD) in reaction to the growing population of illegal aliens. The order states that officers "shall not initiate police action where the objective is to discover the alien status of a person."[1] For officers, this means that they are not allowed to question a person's immigrant status until that person is charged with some other crime.

- In Los Angeles, 95 percent of all outstanding homicide warrants (approximately 1,200 to 1,500) are for illegal aliens.

- Up to 66 percent of fugitive felony warrants (17,000) are for illegal aliens.

- Of the estimated 20,000 members of the 18th Street Gang in California, 60 percent are illegal aliens.

Colorado congressman Tom Tancredo explained sanctuary laws by saying:

> Cities across the land, because of local pressure, because of a variety of reasons, have passed laws, statutes, provisions that restrict their own employees specifically and often the police departments from sharing information with the INS.
>
> … if you in fact stop or arrest someone and … that person is here illegally, you cannot tell the INS. … You cannot aid the Immigration and Naturalization Service in upholding the law and enforcing the law, telling actual police departments to not aid in the enforcement of our law.[2]

Mexican Mafia Connection

The 18th Street Gang works with the Mexican Mafia, which is a force in California prisons. The gang is involved in drug distribution, extortion, and drive-by shootings. They are also responsible for an average of one robbery or assault every day.

Suburban police can now act as immigration agents. Section 287(g)

is attached to the Immigration and
Nationality Act of 1996. This section
gives local and state officers the
ability to enforce immigration with
proper training and federal
supervision. This voluntary program
is being utilized by local police
departments around the country.

"Traffic stops are for safety
and not for enforcing immigration."[4]

—Monique Bond,
Chicago police
spokeswoman

ILLEGAL IMMIGRANTS AND THE POLICE

In December 2006, the Police Department of
Carpentersville, Illinois, joined the Section 287(g)
federal program. Police Chief Dave Neumann said that
officers would only use the power to identify illegal
immigrants who are accused of serious crimes. But, not
everyone in Carpentersville believes that. Linda
Ramirez Sliwinski is a Carpentersville Trustee and the
only official who voted against the program. She said,

> Our village with [the federal training] is like putting a gun
> in the hands of children. I'm afraid that some of our police
> officers will use it to do more racial profiling.[3]

One negative effect of this program is that it can
make illegal aliens (who are not criminals otherwise)
afraid to report crimes and contact the police. Angeles

Ortega-Moore is the executive director of the Latin American Coalition in Charlotte, North Carolina.

Sanctuary Policies

A sanctuary is a place someone can go for protection and immunity from the law. With the increase in the number of illegal immigrants, some cities have informal sanctuary policies to protect illegal aliens.

In Los Angeles, for example, city employees and police cannot cooperate or offer information regarding illegal aliens to the federal immigration service. Other cities that offer some form of sanctuary include Chicago, New York City, San Francisco, and Seattle. By eliminating the threat of being reported to the immigration authorities, these cities believe they will gain the cooperation of the illegal aliens in reporting crimes.

As illegal immigrants have become aware of which cities offer sanctuary, those cities have experienced an increase in illegal immigrant population. Those cities have also experienced the loss of blue collar workers whose jobs may have been lost to the illegal aliens, who will accept lower pay.

According to the FAIR (Federation for American Immigration Reform) organization,

> With an estimated 9–11 million illegal aliens ... and fewer than 2,000 ... immigration agents ... sanctuary policies seriously hamper efforts to harness local police capabilities in augmenting federal enforcement of immigration laws.[6]

While she supports deportation of criminals, she says the program "creates chaos ... People are fearful that someone may come knocking on our door."[5]

ILLEGAL IMMIGRANTS ARE NOT CRIMINALS

Studies also show immigrants are less likely to be criminals than native-born Americans. Rubén G. Rumbaut is a professor of Sociology at the University of

California at Irvine. He cites several studies based on the Children of Immigrants Longitudinal Study (CILS) that prove this point.

Rumbaut states that Mexican immigrants were only one-fourth as likely to go to prison as American-born individuals. These rates were lowest among the least educated, undocumented Latin American immigrants. Rumbaut considers this to be an interesting point. Usually, it is the lack of education among illegal aliens that is blamed for their involvement in crime. He also notes that the lack of education does have an effect on the likelihood that people will end up in jail. But, the effect is greater on people who were born in America than those who are recent immigrants.

Rumbaut also found that the rates of imprisonment increased with the second and third generations (those who had parents or grandparents originally from Mexico). The study shows that the longer immigrants have lived in the United States, the higher their rate of imprisonment. Rambaut reports that of all ethnic groups of undocumented immigrants, foreign-born Mexican men have nearly the lowest rate of imprisonment.

There are many predictors of future imprisonment. These include a family divorce, grade point average, school suspension, level of education, drugs, or a physical threat. These factors are more likely to lead to imprisonment than being of Mexican descent.

Research affirmed that emigrants to the United States were far less likely to become involved in the criminal justice system than second- and third-generation descendants.

A study by the Immigration Policy Center finds that regardless of ethnicity, immigrants have the lowest incarceration rate among young men. This includes the less educated as well. Data cites a 34 percent decline in violent crime since 1994 while the number of illegal immigrants has doubled. Crime is an issue in the United States, but it does not appear to be created or increased by illegal immigration.

Hispanic students attend a college course offered in a high school.

Governor Arnold Schwarzeneggar recognizes that the large number of immigrants in California impacts the economy as well as social services and health care costs.

Social Services, Health Care, and the Costs

D o social services, public school education, and uninsured health care for illegal immigrants cost taxpayers money? Does cheap labor come with high costs? This is another illegal immigration issue.

SOCIAL SERVICES COST CITIZENS MONEY

Opponents of illegal immigration believe that illegal immigrants do cost taxpayers significant amounts of money. Steven Camarota is the director of research at the Center for Immigration Studies. He believes that illegal immigrants cost taxpayers money because they are unskilled, not because they are illegal. Because 60 percent of illegal immigrants lack a high school diploma, they pay little in taxes due to their earning potential. What impact would be felt if the illegal immigrants living in the United States today were granted amnesty? Camarota's research suggests those costs would triple because illegal immigrants would have increased access to social services and other programs.

In Camarota's report, "The High Cost of Cheap Labor," he states that undocumented immigrants produce:

- An annual deficit of $2.5 billion in Medicaid.

- $2.2 billion in emergency room costs.

- $1.9 billion in food assistance program costs.

- $1.6 billion in justice system costs.

- $1.4 billion in education costs.

California has the greatest number of illegal immigrants in the country. California also is finding it financially difficult to deal with its changing population. In Orange County, half of the public-assistance program caseloads are made up of illegal immigrant families. Aid given to families with dependent children grew by 76 percent between 1986 and 1991.

HEALTH CARE COSTS AFFECT CITIZENS

Studies show that the health care system is affected by illegal immigration. In Texas, New Mexico, Arizona, and California, dozens of hospitals have faced bankruptcy or closing because federal programs enforce emergency room care for illegal immigrants.

A FAIR report states that some border hospitals have reported losses of $190 million in costs that have not been reimbursed for treating illegal aliens in 2000. Medical services for illegal immigrants amount to $1,183 per native household.

Madeleine Pelner Cosman, Ph.D., has written an article for the

"The question taxpayers keep asking is 'why should we pay for services for those who have broken the law to get here?' They should not, nor should they be forced to be the Health Maintenance Organization (HMO) and School District of the world. This is evidenced in every poll I have seen indicating that every ethnic group is opposed to illegal immigration and supports enforcement of the law."[1]

—Michael Antonovitch, Los Angeles County supervisor, 5th district

Illegal immigrant students receive help from a federally funded program.

Journal of American Physicians and Surgeons. She writes,

> *What is unseen is their [illegal immigrants] free medical care that has degraded and closed some of America's finest emergency medical facilities, and caused hospital bank- ruptcies: 84 California hospitals are closing their doors.* [2]

In addition, Cosman writes about the issue of "anchor babies." This term is used to describe babies born to illegal immigrants in American hospitals. Any baby born in the United States is automatically a U.S. citizen. The term "anchor" is used because the baby becomes the family's legal foothold in the United States. The baby's family qualifies for public welfare aid. Between 300,000 and 350,000 anchor babies are born each year. In 2003, at the San Joaquin General Hospital's maternity ward in California, 70 percent of the 2,300 babies born were of illegal immigrant parents. In 1994, the cost of 74,987 births of anchor babies in California was $215 million.

California: A Closer Look

California has the highest percentage of illegal immigrants—at a huge cost to California taxpayers. The Federation for American Immigration Reform (FAIR) created a report on the costs of illegal immigrants. The following education, health care, and incarceration information applies to California.

- **Education: $7.7 billion a year**
  Approximately 15 percent of K–12 public school students are children of illegal immigrants.

- **Health care: $1.4 billion a year**
  Costs that medical facilities pay that are not reimbursed.

- **Incarceration: $1.4 billion a year**
  Costs the state pays for imprisonment (jail or prison). This does not include legal costs or the money lost due to the crime.

ILLEGAL IMMIGRANTS CONTRIBUTE TO THE ECONOMY

Other studies suggest that illegal immigrants are not a burden to U.S. taxpayers. Research from the Urban Institute states that "undocumented men come to the United States almost exclusively to work."[3] In 2003, over 90 percent of undocumented men worked. This is a higher rate than that of U.S. citizens and legal immigrants. The suggestion has been made that illegal immigrants come to the United States to receive welfare. However, illegal immigrants are ineligible for welfare, food stamps, Medicaid, and other public benefits.

"If you look at the hospitals, especially in those border states, many have closed down or are on the verge of collapsing, due in large part to the health care they are required to provide by law to illegal immigrants."[4]

—Yeh Ling-Ling,
executive director of
Diversity Alliance for a
Sustainable America in
Oakland

This research also reports that illegal immigrants pay substantial taxes. They pay real estate taxes, whether through home ownership or through taxes passed on by rents. They pay the same sales and consumption taxes as everyone else. These taxes fund the majority of state and local costs of schooling and other services. Also, the U.S. Social Security Administration estimated that 75 percent of illegal immigrants pay payroll taxes. And, a portion of their pay accounts for between $6 billion and $7 billion in Social Security funds that they cannot claim. In this way, "Illegal immigrants were responsible for

Medical

A Rand Corporation study shows that 68 percent of the 664 illegal immigrants in the study were uninsured. Only 19 percent had serious medical conditions, compared with 38 percent of adults born in the United States. Approximately 58 percent of illegal immigrants saw a doctor in the previous year; 80 percent of adults born in the United States saw a doctor in the previous year.

10 percent of the government's surplus in 2004."[5]

Carole Keeton Strayhorn is a former Texas Comptroller. The comptroller's office is responsible for collecting state revenues and tracking expenses. During her term as the Texas Comptroller, a special report showed that undocumented workers helped the Texas economy. They contributed more to the economy than they received in social services.

In the report, Strayhorn states:

> The absence of the estimated 1.4 million undocumented immigrants in Texas in fiscal 2005 would have been a loss to our gross state product of $17.7 billion. Undocumented immigrants produced $1.58 billion in state revenues, which exceeded the $1.16 billion in state services they received.[6]

Many Hospital Patients Are Uninsured

Hospitals regularly deal with uninsured patients, both illegal immigrants and legal residents. For hospitals though, the main concern is treating patients who need to be treated. Dr. Ron Anderson is associated with Parkland Health and Hospital System in Dallas.

Doctor with patient

In an *AMNews* article, Anderson commented on
Parkland's role when dealing with illegal immigrants.
He says that Parkland legally cannot and does not
discriminate between illegal immigrants and citizens.
Anderson believes that doctors have an oath to care for
people, regardless of their legal status; only the federal
government can enforce immigration law.

Jan Emerson, a spokeswoman for the California Hospital Association, states that, "It is unfair for the public to place blame for all of societal ills—in this case, hospital ills—on undocumented or illegal immigrants."[7] Emerson adds that the majority of the 46 million uninsured people in the United States are legal residents or native born.

⚹Added Education Expenses

Orange County, California, is required to pay to have classes taught in Spanish for the 75 percent of students in Santa Ana who are labeled as having low English skills or Limited English Proficiency (LEP). This increases the per-pupil cost by 50 percent.

Public colleges in ten states offer in-state tuition rates to illegal immigrants. A bill to penalize these colleges is being debated in the U.S. House of Representatives and the U.S. Senate. Under this bill, public colleges and universities could lose significant federal funding if they use federal dollars to support these policies.

We're Everywhere

Jessica Vasquez, a student preparing to graduate from Chicago State College, said, "I haven't even told some of my closest friends that I'm an 'illegal.' I'm embarrassed. People have so many ideas about who undocumented people are. You know, usually a landscaper or somebody working in a field. They don't think of us as students or anything else, but really we're everywhere."[8]

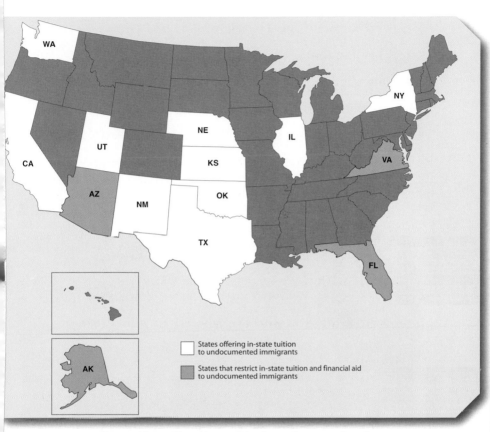

States with specific tuition policies for undocumented workers

The ten states offering in-state tuition to undocumented immigrants are California, Illinois, Kansas, Nebraska, New Mexico, New York, Oklahoma, Texas, Utah, and Washington. Laws passed in Alaska, Arizona, Florida, and Virginia restrict in-state tuition and financial aid for undocumented immigrants.

EDUCATION AND CITIZENSHIP

A bill called the DREAM Act would allow undocumented students to earn citizenship if they pursue higher education and meet other standards. This bill has passed in the U.S. Senate. Senator Richard J. Durbin, who co-sponsors the bill, said:

> *They are American in every sense except their technical legal status. They are honor roll students, star athletes, talented artists and valedictorians. They also are tomorrow's doctors, nurses, teachers, policemen, firefighters, soldiers, and senators.* [9]

Students Andres Garcia, left, and Gaby Pacheco support the American Dream Act. The act would grant in-state tuition to immigrant students who are not residents of the United States.

Migrant farm workers picking strawberries

EMPLOYMENT, WAGES, AND UNDOCUMENTED WORKERS

A central issue in the illegal immigration debate is the effect undocumented workers have on employment and wage levels. There is a concern that illegal immigrants drive wage levels down when they are willing to work for less. Therefore, groups feel that undocumented workers are taking jobs away from Americans who refuse to accept low wages. Others feel that undocumented workers are accepting unskilled jobs that go unfilled by American workers. Some employers are concerned that their industries will suffer if their undocumented workers are forced to leave the country. There is convincing evidence for both sides of this argument.

NEGATIVE EFFECTS ON THE JOB MARKET

Professor Peter Cappelli from the University of Pennsylvania's Wharton Business School and Vernon M. Briggs of the Cornell Business School coauthored an article in May 2006 for *Knowledge@Wharton.* They wrote that undocumented workers reduce wages and diminish work opportunities for low-skilled American workers.

Briggs states that, typically, undocumented workers are males between the ages of 18 and 30 and will take almost any job. This includes situations in which they may be exploited. Illegal immigrants who do not understand U.S. employment

Huddle Study

Dr. Donald Huddle is a Rice University economics professor. The Huddle study is an analysis of the cost of illegal immigrants. The 1996 Huddle study states that illegal immigrants displace, or drive out, almost 730,000 American workers every year at a cost of $4.3 billion annually.

laws and cannot turn to the police for help are often exploited by employers. Briggs states that "if we don't get serious about enforcing [immigration laws], people are going to continue to be hurt. These are the most vulnerable members of society."[1]

Briggs also states that the most effective way to stop illegal immigration is by imposing severe consequences for employers who violate the law. He says:

That means [instituting] heavy penalties on employers who hire immigrants and making it clear that illegal immigrants are not going to work. They are not

Farm Workers

U.S. farmers are facing labor shortages. Federal raids have increased. Illegal farm workers are being deported in growing numbers.

In October 2006, a western New York farmer lost 28 workers in a raid. In another raid, a farmer lost six of his ten employees. Raids are causing a climate of fear in farming communities.

Mary Jo Dudley directs the Cornell Farmworker Program. She says, "It serves as a polarizing force in communities. The immigrant workers … see anyone as a potential enemy. The growers are nervous . … There's this environment of fear and mistrust ."[2]

The American Farm Bureau Federation warns that labor shortages could cause $5 billion in losses to the agriculture industry. The Farm Credit Associations of New York also suggest that New York could lose more than 900 farms in the next two years because of labor shortages.

Farmers in Pennsylvania are pushing for guest-worker program reform. This would allow seasonal workers to come to the United States without risk of deportation. A local farmer who depends on three foreign workers at his farm said, "If they're gone tomorrow, everything basically stops. We can't get it all done ourselves."[3]

supposed to be here; they will gradually get the idea they have to go back, that there's not much hope they are going to get legalized status.[4]

Another factor in the employment issue is that identification is required for many jobs. This fuels the market for fake Social Security and permanent residency cards. Illegal immigrants can buy these cards for less than $100 in Phoenix, Arizona. The cards are so realistic that it is difficult for anyone other than an expert to recognize the card as a fake. In addition, identity theft can be big business for people involved in these false identification schemes.

Working Illegally

Eliseo, an illegal immigrant, describes his experience of illegally working for a cleaning company:

"I entered the United States with an offer of a good job from the owner of a cleaning company, who was the brother of one of my friend[s] from Mexico. ... The owner of the company never explained our job thoroughly we were working seven days a week, without any days off. We were entitled two days off a 'year' (thanksgiving and Christmas) . ... On thanksgiving day ... we did not have to work at the restaurant, but we still had our chores to do, we had to clean the house because the owner had a family coming over for the holidays."[5]

UNDOCUMENTED WORKERS ARE ESSENTIAL WORKERS

On the other side of this debate is the argument that undocumented workers are essential workers in the U.S. economy. Bernard Anderson, a professor at Wharton and a former Assistant Secretary of Labor, disagrees with Briggs in the Wharton Business School article.

Anderson believes the evidence shown by economists is mixed. He states:

> We have to recognize that the huge numbers [of undocumented workers in the United States] are not here to receive welfare; they are here to work. If there were no employment opportunities for them, they wouldn't be coming.[6]

In the same article, Jeffrey S. Passel of the Pew Hispanic Center argues:

> The presence of illegals is not associated with higher unemployment among natives .... Geographically, it tends to be the reverse: Places with large numbers of illegals tend to have lower unemployment than places without illegals. Illegals go where the economies are strong, and as a result there's no impact.[7]

"There is a rational middle ground between granting an automatic path to citizenship for every illegal immigrant and a program of mass deportation. That middle ground recognizes that there are differences between an illegal immigrant who crossed the border recently and someone who has worked here for many years and has a home, a family and an otherwise clean record."[8]

—President George W. Bush

As more American citizens and legal residents are becoming highly educated and aging, more low-skilled jobs become available. In 2007, the United States distributed 5,000 visas for foreign workers in less-skilled occupations.

Taking the oath of U.S. citizenship

Benjamin Johnson, Director of Immigration Policy of the American Immigration Lawyers Association, states that:

> ... we essentially have no legal channels of employment-based immigration for these workers, they either come here illegally or they attempt to come through the already

"We must also recognize that both the United States and Mexico have historically benefited from Mexicans obtaining employment in the United States. A number of our States have special labor needs, and we should take this into account. Illegal immigrants in considerable numbers have become productive members of our society and are a basic part of our work force. Those who have established equities in the United States should be recognized and accorded legal status. At the same time, in so doing, we must not encourage illegal immigration."[11]

—*President Ronald Reagan*

overburdened family–based system. In this environment everybody loses. Families are separated and workers are expected to wait years for jobs that are available today.[9]

Unauthorized workers find jobs in many occupations. They find work in farming, construction, landscaping, cleaning, and food preparation. Undocumented workers who are day laborers find work by waiting in the parking lots of hardware stores. Landscapers or contractors drive by and offer jobs for the day.

Juan Barrera, an undocumented worker, said, "I want to offer what I have to this country, which is my labor. All we want is to work."[10]

Waiting for work

A newer fence runs along the original fence on the U.S.-Mexico border. San Diego, California, is on the left and Tijuana, Mexico, is on the right.

SECURING THE BORDER: FENCE OR NO FENCE

*I*mmigration reform includes the need for a way to stop illegal immigrants from crossing the border. Building a border fence is one solution. But even among those against illegal immigration, a border fence has mixed support.

BORDER FENCE WILL INCREASE SECURITY

The Secure Fence Act passed in 2006 authorized hundreds of miles of additional fencing along the southern border of the United States. President George W. Bush said, "This bill will help protect the American people. This bill will make our borders more secure. It is an important step towards immigration reform."[1]

Jay Ting, a professor at the Temple University Law School, wrote that every day, thousands of people from foreign countries will successfully walk into the United States as long as there is no effective border fence in place. Ting believes that a country with advanced technology should realize that building a fence is the main solution to securing the southern border. He acknowledges that a fence may be costly. However, it is much less expensive than more prisons, border patrol agents, immigration judges, and surveillance equipment, he says.

The We Need a Fence group believes that a fence is the right step toward the solution to illegal immigration. According to the We Need a Fence Web site, the group recognizes that the United States is a nation of immigrants. The group is

"This country has lost control of its borders, and no country can sustain that kind of position."[2]

—*President Ronald Reagan*

not against immigration. They are against illegal immigration. They suggest that before immigration reform can be put in place, a security fence must be built to secure the southern U.S. border.

Minuteman Project

The Minuteman Project, Inc. is a voluntary citizens group founded in 2004. It is dedicated to reducing illegal border crossings into the United States. The group took its name from the Minutemen soldiers in the American Revolution who claimed to be ready to fight in one minute.

The main activity of the Minuteman Project is to watch the border and report sightings of illegal border crossings to the United States Border Patrol. Members have put up fencing on private property in sections of the southern border of the United States. They have also been involved in political protests against illegal immigration.

President Bush called the members vigilantes, or people who take the law into their own hands. Mexican President Vicente Fox has criticized the members as racists. Some American human rights activists have accused that members include white supremacists. Jim Gilchrist is the founder of the Minuteman Project. In order to keep out racists, Gilchrist says he does careful background checks of people who apply to join.

Members argue that they have many African-American members. One African-American member, Ted Hayes, said that many minorities believe undocumented immigrants are taking American jobs and keeping wages low.

The fence has also gained support from Democrats in the U.S. Senate. New York Senator Hilary Clinton supports a high-technology fence that could detect people approaching it from a distance of 200–300 yards (180–300 m). She has also stated that the placement of surveillance drones and infrared cameras might be a good idea.

The Opposite Side of the Fence

There are groups who believe building a border fence is an ineffective, expensive, and impractical proposal to secure the U.S. border.

High-tech Surveillance

A surveillance drone is operated remotely. It can use heat and night-vision equipment to help border guards keep watch over an area. Infrared cameras can capture images at night and during poor weather conditions.

In a small town in Arizona, where citizens face the issue of illegal immigration every day, the border fence is a sensitive issue. Jim Pederson is a former president of the Arizona Democratic Party. His concern is that illegal immigrants can find ways to go around, under, or over a fence. A better solution is needed, he believes.

The United States shares a 2,000-mile (3,000-km) border with Mexico. The Secure Fence Act supports building 700 miles (1,000 km) of fence along the most vulnerable sections of the border. This would leave 1,300 miles (2,000 km) of the border still open. The bill was approved prior to the November 2006 elections. Some people believe the $1.2 billion fencing bill was approved as a gesture to show that the government was moving toward some version of immigration reform.

Two months after approving the fence, the U.S. Senate was set to vote on providing the funds. Moments before the final vote, a provision was added. The provision required the United States to consult with the Mexican government before building the fence. This could delay building the fence for years. Former Justice Department official Kris Kobach, in a statement to the House Subcommittee, said:

> *I know of no other provision in U.S. law where the federal government requires state and local government on the border—to consult with state and local governments of a foreign power before the federal government can act. … If you add this, three levels of government and foreign power, your delay will never end.[3]*

In the final vote, the U.S. Senate voted against providing the funds to build the fence. Senator Jeff Sessions said:

> *We will rightly be accused of not being serious about the commitments we've made to the American people with regard to actually enforcing the laws of immigration in America, which many Americans already believe we are not serious about. They don't respect what we've done in the past, and they should not. We have failed, and it's time for us to try to fix it and do better.[4]*

"The Congress should abandon the fence. … It flies in the face of America as a symbol of freedom."[5]

—Bill Richardson, Governor of New Mexico

The Secure Fence Act authorized approximately 700 miles of fencing on the U.S.-Mexico border.

Other groups oppose the border fence as well. Native communities have threatened legal action to prevent the fence from dividing their grazing and farming land. Ecological groups also oppose the fence, stating it will harm the environment. They will use every means available to prevent it from being built.

Others believe that building a border fence is impractical. It would only lead illegal immigrants to cross in the areas not protected by the fence. Former U.S. Customs agents consider it almost impossible to build a fence along the mountains and deserts of the Arizona border due to the rough terrain.

One former agent pointed out that the fence would have to bridge hundreds of creek beds that are prone to flash flooding on the Arizona border. He said:

> You are going to have to build hundreds of culverts big enough for debris the size of brush and small trees to float through the length of the border. If it is wide enough for bushes to get through, then people can get through.[6]

Many people believe that the fence might slow down illegal immigration in the specific areas where the fence is built. But they also believe it is a limited solution to the problem. Doris Meissner of the Migration Policy Institute sums it up by saying:

> It may work to curtail crossings in the immediate area it has been built, but it won't stop illegal immigration. ... The draw for illegal immigrants is the availability of employment in the United States, and that is not being addressed by this fence.[7]

Men walk along the Mexican side of the fence, waiting for the opportunity to cross illegally into the United States from Tijuana, Mexico.

A Day Without Immigrants protest in Chicago

Out from the Shadows

Typically, illegal immigrants have lived
under the radar of police and authorities.
This is often referred to as "living in the shadows."
Illegal immigrants who want to stay in the country
try to live quietly in the background.

A December 2006 article in *The New York Times* chronicled the life of an illegal immigrant named Verónica. In south-central Texas, Border Patrol agents regularly monitor the main roads. She tries to get around on side streets. An informal network of friends and family alert her to areas she should avoid. Verónica avoids contact with neighbors. She says,

> *You never know. There are bad people in the world. We could have a problem with immigration. There is a lot of envy in the world, so we are careful.*[1]

Verónica's story is typical of illegal immigrants trying to blend into communities. This has been the case for many years. Recently, illegal immigrants have emerged from the shadows to protest in large-scale national and local rallies for immigrant rights.

One of the first of these statements was the Immigrant Workers Freedom Ride, which was held September 20 to October 4, 2003. Organized by the hotel and restaurant workers union, the ride took activists through 42 states and 106 cities. The ride ended in a 100,000-person rally in Flushing

"The marches reflect a huge infusion of new people, new talent, and new perspectives."[2]

—Joshua Hoyt, executive director of the Illinois Coalition for Immigrant and Refugee Rights

Meadows, New York. The ride united people from large organizations, labor unions, and churches. For the first time, undocumented workers and their supporters rallied to gain the public's attention.

Immigrant Workers Freedom Ride

The Immigrant Workers Freedom Ride of 2003 was formed to expose the perceived injustice of current U.S. policies toward immigrants. Participants were asking for amnesty for the millions of law-abiding, hardworking, illegal immigrants currently in the United States.

Approximately 1,000 immigrant workers boarded buses in Seattle, Portland, San Francisco, Los Angeles, Las Vegas, Minneapolis, Chicago, Houston, Miami, and Boston. They crossed the country for 12 days before arriving in Washington, D.C. for two days to gain the attention of Congress. The final stop was Flushing Meadows, New York. Approximately 100,000 protestors gathered to rally for the cause of illegal immigrants.

Illegal immigrants and their supporters are fighting for:

- Granting legal status to immigrant workers already established in the United States.
- Clearing the path to citizenship.
- Including illegal immigrant workers in labor protection regulations.
- Streamlining outdated immigration policies to reunite families.
- Respecting the civil rights and civil liberties of all.

A border security bill was proposed in 2006 by the Chairman of the House Judiciary Committee, Jim Sensenbrenner. The bill would make it a felony to be in the United States illegally or to assist someone who is. Outraged Latinos and illegal immigrant workers responded with their own call for action.

Demonstrations against the bill occurred in

Washington, D.C., on March 7,
2006, and in Chicago on March 10.
More than 30,000 protestors
gathered in Washington, D.C.
Organizers had expected only 5,000
protestors. Approximately 100,000
people marched through downtown
Chicago. Approximately 500,000
immigrants and their supporters
marched to Los Angeles City Hall on
March 25. Similarly large protests
occurred in Phoenix, Atlanta, and
Dallas.

"The message is 'Today we march, tomorrow we vote.'"[3]

—Hector Flores, president of the League of United Latin American Citizens

On April 10, 2006, the National Day of Action,
immigrants gathered for rallies across the country.
Approximately 2 million demonstrators rallied in
more than 120 cities in 40 states.

On May 1, 2006, immigrant workers and their
supporters participated in the A Day Without
Immigrants boycott. The largest boycotts occurred in
California, Washington, Oregon, Texas, Arizona,
Florida, and other agricultural areas. The boycott
protested the government's efforts against illegal
immigration. It also raised the awareness of the
importance of immigrants' jobs to the U.S. economy.

Protesters march through downtown San Francisco in support of amnesty for illegal immigrants.

PROTESTS HAVE UNCLEAR RESULTS

The sheer numbers involved in these rallies made a statement. But the statement was not clear. Some protestors carried flags of their native countries. Other protestors shouted in Spanish or sang the national anthem in Spanish.

Tim Chapman, director of the Heritage
Foundation's Center for Media and Public Policy, said:

> In real time those pictures were going up on the Internet as
> part of a message that said this is a movement about being
> bestowed rights that we have in the United States and not
> assimilating, and not even a movement that values Amer-
> ican culture and assimilation.[4]

The protests may have caused some negative effects
on Capitol Hill. Senator Pete Domenici from New
Mexico said:

> I have great respect for a lot of the people that did the
> protesting, but I think their message is all confused. The flag,
> the anthem, all that, it got everybody all mixed up. "Take off
> work"—it sounded wrong to some people, right to others.[5]

The protests have achieved
attention for a situation in America
which needs to be addressed. Frank
Sherry, executive director of the
National Immigration Forum, said:

> Obviously, there's tremendous pres-
> sure on lawmakers to fix the problem.
> The marches in the street, the public

Earlier Freedom Rides

The Immigrant Workers
Freedom Ride was modeled
after the Freedom rides of
1961, as part of the Civil
Rights Movement, which
supported equal rights for
African Americans.

"One of the messages … is that the community is losing that sense that you have to live underground in this society, and is seeing how important it is to raise their voices."[7]

—Alvaro Huerta,
of the Coalition for
Human Immigrant Rights
of Los Angeles

opinion polls that show immigration is one of the top two or three issues in the country. But the crosscurrents of politics and policy are such that it's going to take a tremendous push from President Bush and from Democratic and Republican leaders to get this done.[6]

Protesters gathered on May 1, 2006, in Phoenix, Arizona. The intent of the nationwide boycott was to show the importance of immigrants to the U.S. economy. Immigrants were asked not to work or spend any money on that day.

President Bush, at left, watches a naturalization ceremony
for 29 new U.S. citizens in the Great Hall of New York's Ellis Island.

PROPOSALS FOR
IMMIGRATION REFORM

n estimated 11 to 12 million illegal

immigrants live in the United States.

Many believe that America is in need of immigration

reform. However, it is unclear what exactly needs to be

done and how to move forward. A variety of proposals

use a variety of approaches. These include actions to secure the border. They also include actions to deal with the illegal immigrant population already established in the United States.

In 2007, the U.S. House of Representatives and the U.S. Senate presented competing bills for immigration reform. The House favors a proposal of immigration enforcement and border protection. The U.S. Senate favors a guest-worker program and a path to citizenship for illegal immigrants. The president also has opinions on the issue. So, what does each bill propose? What does the president favor?

"By balancing the needs of families and employers, and by extending a safe haven to those fleeing persecution, our immigration policy serves its historic purpose. Freedom and opportunity is the cornerstone of American society, and immigrants continue to embody that freedom."[1]

—Senator Spencer Abraham, December 3, 1996

U.S. HOUSE OF REPRESENTATIVES

The proposed House bill focuses on border security and law enforcement. The bill calls for a border fence in certain areas on the U.S. border with Mexico. This bill:

- Makes it a felony to be an illegal immigrant or assist an illegal immigrant.

- Makes employers responsible for checking the legal status of workers.

- Increases fines for employers who hire illegal immigrants.

- Requires detention for illegal immigrants caught at the border and jail time for smugglers.

- Requires building a fence along 700 miles (1,000 km) of the U.S.-Mexican border.

U.S. SENATE

The proposed Senate bill focuses on some fence building on the border as well as increased border patrol. It also opens paths for some illegal immigrants to gain citizenship or other legal residency. This bill:

- Allows illegal immigrants, who have been in the country for five years, a path to citizenship. Illegal immigrants would pay fines, back taxes, and fees, and learn English.

- Requires illegal immigrants who have been living in the United States for two to five years to return to the border and file an application to return to the United States.

- Illegal immigrants who have been in the country for less than two years would be required to leave the country.

- Requires that illegal immigrants who are convicted of a felony crime or three misdemeanor crimes be removed from the United States.

- Creates a guest-worker program for 1.5 million farm workers and provides a path to permanent residency.

- Increases temporary guest-worker visas and employment-based Green Cards.

- Increases border patrol and requires building 370 miles (595 km) of fencing along the border.

- Requires employers to check status of workers.

- Increases fines for employers who hire illegal immigrants.

- Declares English the country's national language.

The President

President George W. Bush favors a guest-worker

program that does not provide a path to legal residency. He suggests that 6,000 National Guard troops be sent to the border. The President has signed the Secure Fence Act that provides for 700 miles (1,126 km) of fencing along the border.

Finding Middle Ground

There are similarities in the House and Senate bills, such as a border fence and increased border patrol. But, there are also some key differences. The House and the Senate differ on the ways to treat existing illegal immigrants in the United States. The House would treat illegal immigrants as criminals. The Senate would offer most illegal immigrants a route to citizenship and legal residency.

Can a guest-worker program without a path to permanent residency work? In an article in the *Washington Post,* Tamar Jacoby writes:

> There is nothing more permanent than a temporary worker. Many of those who come to the United States for short stints will want to stay on after their visas expire, perpetuating the underground economy that the program is supposed to eliminate.[2]

The road to immigration reform is rough at the moment as seen by the dividing opinions in our government. How illegal immigrants who are living in the United States will be treated is the most controversial part of the issue. Zoe Lofgren, who heads the House Judiciary panel on immigration, thinks the bills can be worked out. Lofgren said, "If we stop yelling at each other and just calmly and methodically work through the issues ...we'll come up with a practical bill that will work and will last."[3]

IMMIGRATION REFORM BILL NEEDS REFORM

In 2007, the U.S. Senate created a bill to address the issues of illegal immigrants and undocumented workers. The bill proposed to tighten border security and create a path to citizenship for about 12 million illegal immigrants.

On June 28, 2007, the Senate voted on whether or not it should limit debate and move to voting on the proposed bill. The Senate members voted 46 in favor and 53 against. A vote of 60 in favor was needed to end debate and vote on the bill. The vote was not along party lines—members of each party voted for and against moving the bill along.

Members of both political parties agreed on a mandatory verification system and tamper-proof cards for undocumented workers. In general, the Democrats who voted against moving the current bill along wanted even more protection for illegal immigrants. The Republicans who voted against it were concerned the bill would lead to amnesty for all illegal immigrants.

The American public made its feelings known. Citizens voiced their opinions by calling and e-mailing their senators in record numbers. A survey by Rassmussen Reports found that only 23 percent of Americans supported the bill. Other surveys showed that the majority of those polled wanted immigration reform that would remove individuals who entered the country illegally, make English the national language,

"Throughout our history, immigrants have come to America, established themselves and been joined by other members of their families. That process has brought us energetic individuals and strong families who have enriched our economy and way of life."[5]

—Stuart Anderson, Director of Trade and International Studies

and create a mandatory verification system for all employers. For the time being, the immigration reform bill is on hold. It is highly unlikely that another immigration bill will be presented during the Bush administration.

A protestor waves a poster proclaiming his love for the United States. A crowd of mostly Hispanic workers listens to speakers who support U.S. immigration reform that helps reunite families and improve working conditions.

TIMELINE

1808	1882	1891
Ellis Island is sold to the federal government for $10,000 to be used as the site of a fort.	The Chinese Exclusion Act, the first major immigration legislation, passes on May 6.	The Immigration Act of 1891 sets up the first comprehensive law to control immigration and direct deportation.

1924	1954	1965
National Origins Act of 1924 establishes and institutes a quota system and numerical limit on immigration on May 26.	Ellis Island as an immigration station closes on November 29.	The Immigration and Nationality Act of 1965 ends the quota system and sets a uniform limit of 20,000 immigrants per each country.

1892

First immigrants pass through the newly opened Ellis Island immigration station on January 1.

1907

Ellis Island admits 11,747 immigrants on April 17—the most immigrants on any one day.

1917

Illiterate immigrants are excluded from the United States.

1980

The Refugee Act of 1980 sets up the first system and procedure for admitting refugees to the United States.

1986

The Immigration Reform and Control Act passes on November 6.

1990

The Immigration Act of 1990, which allows for increased immigration, passes on November 29.

TIMELINE

1994	**1996**	**2003**
Proposition 187 is approved in California on November 8. Immigrants are ineligible for public services.	The Illegal Immigration Reform and Immigration Responsibilty Act passes on April 24.	The Immigrant Workers Freedom Ride occurs September 30 to October 4.

2006	**2006**	**2006**
A demonstration for immigrant rights takes place in Los Angeles on March 25.	Immigrants and supporters rally for the National Day of Action on April 10.	A Day Without Immigrants raises an awareness of immigrants' jobs to the U.S. economy on May 1.

2005

A border security bill proposed by Jim Sensenbrenner passes on December 16.

2006

A demonstration for immigrant rights occurs in Washington, D.C. on March 7.

2006

A demonstration for immigrant rights is held in Chicago on March 10.

2006

The Secure Fence Act, which focuses on the U.S.-Mexican border, passes on October 26.

2006

Immigrations and Customs Enforcement agents raid Swift & Company meatpacking plants on December 12.

ESSENTIAL FACTS

AT ISSUE

Opposed

❖ Illegal immigration is just that—illegal. Entry through illegal means should not provide a path to citizenship. State tax dollars should not be used to cover the illegal immigrants' costs for public social services, health care, and education.

❖ The Federation for American Immigration (FAIR) promotes the reform of immigration policies and a secure border.

❖ Americans for Legal Immigration does not support amnesty programs or any programs that "short cut" the legal immigration process.

In Favor

❖ Illegal immigrants can bypass the route to U.S. citizenship as their cheap labor contributes to the U.S. economy.

❖ Manufacturing, agriculture, and hospitality industries favor cheap labor.

CRITICAL DATES

November 6, 1986
The Immigration Reform and Control Act addressed illegal immigration.

April 24, 1996
The Illegal Immigration Reform and Immigrant Responsibility Act passed. It emphasized enforcement of and penalties for violating immigration law.

May 1, 2006
Boycotts on A Day Without Immigrants raised awareness of the importance of immigrants' jobs to the U.S. economy.

Quotes

Opposed

"Violations of our immigration laws and privacy rights often go hand in hand. Enforcement actions ... protect the privacy rights of innocent Americans while striking a blow against illegal immigration."—*Michael Chertoff, Secretary of Homeland Security*

In Favor

It's time for the federal government to stop victimizing workers and reform our immigration system. ... America deserves a humane, systematic and comprehensive immigration policy immediately."—*Mark Lauritsen, international vice president and director of the Food Processing, Packing, and Manufacturing division of the UFCW*

ADDITIONAL RESOURCES

SELECT BIBLIOGRAPHY

Curran, Thomas J. *Xenophobia and Immigration, 1820–1930*. Boston: Twain Publishers, 1975.

Daniels, Roger. *Guarding the Golden Door*. New York: Hill and Wang, 2004.

Handlin, Oscar. *A Pictoral History of Immigration*. New York: Crown Publishers, Inc., 1972.

Hayworth, J. D. *Whatever It Takes: Illegal Immigration, Border Security, and the War on Terror*. Washington, D.C.: Regenery Publishing, Inc., 2006.

Hoefer, Michael, Nancy Rytina, and Christopher Campbell. *Estimates of the Unauthorized Immigrant Population Residing in the United States: January 2005*. Department of Homeland Security, Office of Immigration Statistics, Population Estimates report. Aug. 2006.

Kennedy, John F. *A Nation of Immigrants*. New York: Harper & Row, Publishers, Inc., 1964.

Strayhorn, Carole Keeton. Special Report. *Undocumented Immigrants in Texas: A Financial Analysis of the Impact to the State Budget and Economy*. Dec. 2006.

FURTHER READING

Ashabranner, Brent K. *Our Beckoning Borders: Illegal Immigration to America*. New York: Cobblehill Books, 1996.

De Capua, Sarah. *How People Immigrate*. New York: Children's Press, 2004.

Goldish, Meish. *Immigration: How Should It Be Controlled*. New York: Twenty-First Century Books, 1994.

Hauser, Pierre, and Sandra Stotsky. *Illegal Aliens*. Philadelphia: Chelsea House, 1996.

Web Links

To learn more about illegal immigration, visit ABDO Publishing Company on the World Wide Web at **www.abdopublishing.com.** Web sites about illegal immigration are featured on our Book Links page. These links are routinely monitored and updated to provide the most current information available.

Places to Visit

Ellis Island Immigration Museum
National Park Service, Statue of Liberty National Monument, and Ellis Island, New York, NY 10004
212-344-0996
www.ellisisland.com
Ellis Island Immigration Station was the entrance point to America for millions of immigrants between 1892 and 1954.

The Lower East Side Tenement Museum
108 Orchard Street, New York, NY 10002
212-982-8420
www.tenement.org
The Lower East Side Tenement Museum is a preserved tenement building in Manhattan where 7,000 people lived between 1863 and 1935. This landmark tenement building was home to poor immigrant and urban working class people.

National Border Patrol Museum
4315 Trans Mountain Road, El Paso, TX 79924
915-759-6060
www.borderpatrolmuseum.com
This museum explains the history of the U.S. Border Patrol from its beginning in the Old West to today.

GLOSSARY

alien
A foreign national who is not a citizen of the United States. This includes lawful permanent residents (Green Card holders), temporary visa holders, and undocumented foreign nationals.

amnesty
To grant an illegal immigrant citizenship or permanent residency to the United States.

assimilate
To accept and practice the concepts and attitudes of a culture.

asylum
The status sought by a person in the United States with a well-founded fear of persecution if made to return to their country of nationality or last place of residence.

deportation
The process of removing a person from the country for legal reasons.

detainee
A person held in custody.

employer verification
Employers verify the identity and employment authorization of their employees by completing the Form I-9.

fellowship
A position created for advanced study or research.

Green Card
The name of the Alien Registration Receipt Card given to individuals who become legal permanent residents of the United States.

humanitarian
A person who promotes human welfare and social reform.

illegal immigrant
A person who is not legally allowed to live in the United States.

immigrant visa
The document issued to be an eligible, permanent immigrant. The immigrant visa permits entry into the United States as a permanent resident.

indentured servant
A person under contract to an employer to work for a specific amount of time; often in return for passage to another country.

indictment
A formal charge of a legal offense.

legislation
A proposed or enacted law or group of laws.

migrant worker
A person who travels from state to state for work, usually to work on farms.

naturalization
The process by which citizenship is conferred upon a foreign citizen or national.

permanent resident
A non-U.S. citizen who has been given permission to live permanently in the United States.

refugee
A person who is unable or unwilling to return to their country for fear of persecution based on race, religion, nationality, social group, or political opinion.

unauthorized worker
A person who is not legally allowed to work in the United States.

U.S. citizen
A person entitled to the rights, freedoms, and protection of the United States.

U.S. Department of Homeland Security
The goal of the Department of Homeland Security is to preserve and protect America. This includes managing illegal immigration.

U.S. workers
The definition includes U.S. citizens, lawful permanent residents, refugees, those seeking asylum, and temporary residents.

verification
Confirmation for accuracy.

visa
An endorsement made in a passport that allows the specified person to enter the country issuing it.

xenophobia
Fear and hatred of foreigners.

SOURCE NOTES

Chapter 1. A National Raid

1. U.S. Immigration and Customs Enforcement. "U.S. Uncovers Large-Scale Identity Theft Scheme Used By Illegal Aliens to Gain Employment at Nationwide Meat Processor," news release 13 Dec. 2006.

2. White House. "Fact Sheet: Basic Pilot: A Clear and Reliable Way to Verify Employment Eligibility," press release 5 July 2006.

3. Matt McKinney and Gregory A. Patterson. "U.S. Meat Industry Rattled by Raids." *Star Tribune* 14 Dec. 2006.

4. Julia Preston and Martin Forstenzer. "Immigrants' Families Figuring Out What to Do After Federal Raids." *The New York Times* 16 Dec. 2006.

5. United Food and Commercial Workers Union. "ICE Terrorizing Immigrant Workers Because of Failed U.S. Immigration Policy," press release 13 Dec. 2006.

6. U.S. Immigration and Customs Enforcement. "53 former employees at Swift & Company meat processing plant in Cactus, Texas, charged in federal indictments," news release 10 Jan. 2007.

Chapter 2. U.S. Immigration and Legislation

1. Oscar Hardlin,. *A Pictoral History of Immigration.* New York: Crown Publishers, 1972. 28.

2. Emma Lazarus. "The New Colossus." National Park Service U.S. Department of the Interior. 5 Oct. 2006. 28 Mar. 2007 <http://www.nps.gov/stli/historyculture/upload/new%20colossus%20for%20displaypage2.pdf>.

Chapter 3. Who Are Today's Illegal Immigrants?

1. "Advocacy Groups Say U.S. Fails to Protect Illegal Workers." AHN Media Corp. Nov. 2006. 2 July 2007 <http://www.allheadlinenews.com/articles/7005373716>.

2. Elaine Rivera/Ajo. "Mercy Mission In The Desert," TIME." 3 June 2001. 26 June 2007 <http://www.time.com/time/magazine/article/0,9171,128934,00.html?iid=chix-sphere>.

3. Customs and Border Patrol. "CBP Launches Operation Desert Safeguard Aimed at Preventing Migrant Deaths," press release 3 June 2003.

Chapter 4. Xenophobia, Racism, or Concerned Citizens?

1. "Xenophobia." Def. *Webster's New Dictionary.* Third College Edition. 1986.

2. Brenda Walker. "AboutImmigrationsHumanCost." 29 Mar. 2007 <www.immigrationshumancost.org/text/about.html>.

3. FAIR. "300 Million and Counting: Mass Immigration Driving Rapid U.S. Population Growth," news release 18 Oct. 2006.

4. American Friends Service Committee. "National Immigration Opinion Survey Results" 28 June 2007. <http://www.afsc.org/immigration-survey/default.htm>.

Chapter 5. Crime, Drugs, and Illegal Immigrants

1. Los Angeles Police Protective League. "Special Order 40." 12 June 2007 <http://www.lapd.com/article.aspx?a=5285>.

2. Tom Tancredo. "Immigration Problems: Sanctuary Policy and Crime," statement to the U.S. House of Representatives 9 Jul. 2003.

3. John Keilman. "To serve, protect, perhaps deport: Suburb cops could act as immigration agents." *Knight Ridder Tribune Business News*. Washington: 15 Jan. 2007.

4. Ibid.

5. Ibid.

6. Los Angeles Police Protective League. "Special Order 40." 12 June 2007 <http://www.lapd.com/article.aspx?a=5285>.

Chapter 6. Social Services, Health Care, and the Costs

1. Michael D. Antonovich. Remark made on illegal immigration Feb. 1994. *Full Listing of Immigration Quotations. Federation for American Immigration Reform*. 20 Mar. 2007 <http://www.fairus.org/site/PageServer?pagename=research_researche535#antonovich>.

2. Randy Capps and Michael Fix. "Top Six Myths About Undocumented Immigrants." *Registered Nurse: Journal of Patient Advocacy*. July 2006: 21.

3. Victoria Colliver. "Tallying health costs of illegals: Study finds immigrants are not a disproportionate burden." *San Francisco Chronicle*. 15 Nov. 2006.

4. Madeleine Pelner Cosman. "Illegal Aliens and American Medicine." *Journal of American Physicians and Surgeons.* Spring 2005. v. 10, n. 1. 6.

5. Mary Sanchez. "Illegal aliens help subsidize U.S. economy." *Kansas City Star*. 15 Apr. 2005.

6. Carole Keeton Strayhorn. "Undocumented Immigrants in Texas: A Financial Analysis of the Impact to the State Budget and Economy," special report Dec. 2006.

7. Victoria Colliver. "Tallying health costs of illegals: Study finds immigrants are not a disproportionate burden." *San Francisco Chronicle*. 15 Nov. 2006.

8. Kevin Clarke. "These American Lives: Undocumented Stories." *U.S. Catholic*. Aug. 2006: 14.

9. Charles Dervaries. "Congress Takes Up Competing Bills On In-State Tuition for Illegal Immigrants." *Diverse Issues in Higher Education*. 23.11 (2006): 7–7.

Source Notes Continued

Chapter 7. Employment, Wages, and Undocumented Workers

1. "The Immigration Debate: Its Impact on Workers, Wages and Employers Law and Public Policy." *Knowledge@Wharton*. 17 May 2006. 29 Mar. 2007 <http://knowledge.wharton.upenn.edu/article.cfm?articleid=1482&CFID=5397114&CFTOKEN=56228641&jsessionid=9a306c8fd5e62762802d>.

2. Ibid.

3. Nina Bernstein. "Immigrants Go From Farms to Jails, And a Climate of Fear Settles In." *The New York Times*. 24 Dec. 2006.

4. Sharon Smith. "Farmers push guest-worker reform." *The Patriot-News*. 16 Jan. 2007.

5. "Rider Profiles." Immigrant Workers Freedom Ride Coalition. 20 Mar. 2007 <www.iwfr.org/profiles.asp>.

6. "The Immigration Debate: Its Impact on Workers, Wages and Employers Law and Public Policy." Knowledge@Wharton. 17 May 2006. 29 Mar. 2007 <http://knowledge.wharton.upenn.edu/article.cfm?articleid=1482&CFID=5397114&CFTOKEN=56228641&jsessionid=9a306c8fd5e62762802d>.

7. Ibid.

8. Ibid.

9. Benjamin Johnson. Opening statement before the Judiciary Committee on Comprehensive Immigration Reform. U.S. Senate, Washington, D.C. 12 Jul. 2006.

10. Joseph Berger. "Stung In the Search For Work." *The New York Times*. 31 Dec. 2006.

11. Roger Daniels. *Guarding the Golden Door*. New York: Hill and Wang, 2004. 223.

Chapter 8. Securing the Border: Fence or No Fence

1. Office of the Press Secretary. "Fact Sheet: The Secure Fence Act of 2006," press release. 26 Oct. 2006.

2. J.D. Hayworth. *Whatever It Takes: Illegal Immigration, Border Security, and the War on Terror*. Washington, D.C.: Regenery Publishing, Inc., 2006. 176.

3. Charles Hurt. "Senate denies funds for new border fence." *The Washington Times*. 14 July 2006.

4. Ibid.

5. "Richardson Says To GOP: Tear Down That Fence." *Congress Daily* (2006):15–15.

ABOUT THE AUTHOR

Karen Latchana Kenney has written several books for children and young adults. She has a B.A. in English and has been both an editor and an author. Karen lives and works in Minnesota.

PHOTO CREDITS

Wilfredo Lee/AP Images, cover, 3, 98 (bottom); Ed Andrieski/AP Images, 6, 99 (bottom); Khue Bui/AP Images, 11; LM Otero/AP Images, 15; Marty Lederhandler/AP Images, 16, 97 (top); AP Images, 22; Lenny Ignelzi/AP Images, 25; Gregory Bull/AP Images, 26, 97 (bottom); David Maung/AP Images, 31; Humane Borders–HO/AP Images, 35; Denis Poroy/AP Images, 36, 39, 77; Pablo Martinez Monsivais/AP Images, 43; Matt York/AP Images, 44, 69, 87; Charlie Riedel/AP Images, 51; Rich Pedroncelli/AP Images, 52; J.R. Hernandez/AP Images, 55; Karen Kasmauski/Corbis, 59; Lindaanne Donohoe, 61, 72; Alan Diaz/AP Images, 63; Chris O'Meara/AP Images, 64; Lynne Sladky/AP Images, 71; Dario Lopez-Mills/AP Images, 79, 98 (top); Nam Y. Huh/AP Images, 80, 99 (top); Tony Avelar/AP Images, 84; Beth A. Keiser/AP Images, 88; Rogelio Solis/AP Images, 95